5-MINUTE
GRATITUDE
JOURNAL

This Journal Belongs To:

_____

Journal Timeline:

_____

REVIVE *stationery*

5-Minute Gratitude Journal

ISBN: 978-1-83412-140-6

GOALS

TAKE A MOMENT TO ESTABLISH
YOUR GOALS FOR THIS JOURNAL

DESCRIPTION	HABIT	SHORT TERM	MEDIUM TERM	LONG TERM
	☐	☐	☐	☐
	☐	☐	☐	☐
	☐	☐	☐	☐
	☐	☐	☐	☐
	☐	☐	☐	☐
	☐	☐	☐	☐
	☐	☐	☐	☐
	☐	☐	☐	☐
	☐	☐	☐	☐
	☐	☐	☐	☐
	☐	☐	☐	☐
	☐	☐	☐	☐
	☐	☐	☐	☐
	☐	☐	☐	☐
	☐	☐	☐	☐
	☐	☐	☐	☐
	☐	☐	☐	☐

DATE _____

GRATITUDE TURNS WHAT WE HAVE INTO ENOUGH.

WHAT MADE YOU SMILE TODAY?

_____

_____

_____

WHO IS SOMEONE YOU'RE THANKFUL FOR RIGHT NOW?

_____

_____

_____

WHAT IS ONE SIMPLE PLEASURE YOU ENJOYED TODAY?

_____

_____

_____

WHAT MEMORY ARE YOU GRATEFUL FOR TODAY?

_____

_____

_____

WHAT ABILITY OR SKILL DO YOU FEEL THANKFUL FOR TODAY?

_____

_____

_____

APPRECIATION CAN MAKE A DAY—EVEN CHANGE A LIFE.

DATE
_____

GRATITUDE IS NOT ONLY THE GREATEST OF VIRTUES, BUT THE PARENT OF ALL OTHERS.

WHO IS SOMEONE YOU'RE THANKFUL FOR RIGHT NOW?
_____
_____
_____

WHAT IS ONE SIMPLE PLEASURE YOU ENJOYED TODAY?
_____
_____
_____

WHAT MEMORY ARE YOU GRATEFUL FOR TODAY?
_____
_____
_____

WHAT ABILITY OR SKILL DO YOU FEEL THANKFUL FOR TODAY?
_____
_____
_____

WHAT CHALLENGE TAUGHT YOU SOMETHING IMPORTANT?
_____
_____
_____

LET US BE GRATEFUL TO THE PEOPLE WHO MAKE US HAPPY.

DATE _____

GRATITUDE UNLOCKS THE FULLNESS OF LIFE.

WHAT IS ONE SMALL MOMENT FROM TODAY THAT MADE YOU SMILE?

_____

_____

_____

WHO ARE YOU GRATEFUL TO HAVE IN YOUR LIFE AND WHY.

_____

_____

_____

WHAT CHALLENGE TAUGHT YOU SOMETHING YOU ARE THANKFUL FOR?

_____

_____

_____

WHAT IN NATURE ARE YOU MOST THANKFUL FOR TODAY?

_____

_____

_____

WHAT DOES SELF-CARE LOOK LIKE FOR YOU TODAY?

_____

_____

_____

GRATITUDE IS THE FAIREST BLOSSOM
WHICH SPRINGS FROM THE SOUL.

DATE

NO DUTY IS MORE URGENT THAN GIVING THANKS.

WHAT MADE YOU FEEL PROUD OF YOURSELF RECENTLY?

WHAT RECENT CONVERSATION MADE YOU FEEL HEARD OR VALUED?

WHAT PERSONAL STRENGTH ARE YOU MOST GRATEFUL FOR TODAY?

DESCRIBE A MOMENT OF PEACE YOU FOUND OUTDOORS RECENTLY.

WHAT IS A QUIET MOMENT YOU CHERISHED THIS WEEK?

THE MORE GRATEFUL I AM, THE MORE BEAUTY I SEE.

DATE _____

JOY IS THE SIMPLEST FORM OF GRATITUDE.

WHO MADE YOUR DAY BETTER TODAY, AND HOW?
_____
_____
_____

WHO INSPIRES YOU TO BE A BETTER VERSION OF YOURSELF?
_____
_____
_____

IN WHAT WAYS HAVE YOU GROWN OVER THE PAST YEAR?
_____
_____
_____

WHAT'S YOUR FAVORITE SEASON, AND WHAT DO YOU APPRECIATE ABOUT IT?
_____
_____
_____

WHAT DAILY HABIT HELPS YOU STAY GROUNDED?
_____
_____
_____

GRATITUDE MAKES SENSE OF OUR PAST, BRINGS PEACE FOR TODAY, AND CREATES A VISION FOR TOMORROW.

DATE _____

A THANKFUL HEART IS A MAGNET FOR JOY.

WHAT PART OF YOUR ROUTINE ARE YOU MOST THANKFUL FOR?

_____

_____

WHAT LESSON DID SOMEONE TEACH YOU THAT YOU STILL CARRY?

_____

_____

WHAT IS SOMETHING NEW YOU'VE LEARNED THAT IMPROVED YOUR LIFE?

_____

_____

WHAT SENSORY EXPERIENCE FROM NATURE BRINGS YOU JOY?

_____

_____

WHAT BRINGS YOU A SENSE OF CALM DURING STRESSFUL TIMES?

_____

_____

_____

EVEN A CLOUDY DAY CAN HOLD BRIGHT MOMENTS.

DATE

START EACH DAY WITH A GRATEFUL THOUGHT AND WATCH THE MAGIC UNFOLD.

WHAT IS ONE KIND GESTURE SOMEONE DID FOR YOU THIS WEEK?

_____

_____

WHAT SHARED EXPERIENCE ARE YOU THANKFUL FOR?

_____

_____

WHAT PAST MISTAKE HELPED SHAPE WHO YOU ARE NOW?

_____

_____

WHAT PLACE IN THE WORLD ARE YOU MOST THANKFUL TO HAVE VISITED?

_____

_____

WHAT PART OF YOUR HEALTH ARE YOU ESPECIALLY THANKFUL FOR TODAY?

_____

_____

_____

JOY BEGINS WITH THANK YOU.

DATE
_____

APPRECIATION IS A POWERFUL FORM OF ABUNDANCE.

WHAT'S A RECENT ACCOMPLISHMENT YOU FEEL GRATEFUL FOR?
_____
_____
_____

WHAT PART OF YOUR HOME FEELS LIKE A SANCTUARY?
_____
_____
_____

WHAT SIMPLE PLEASURE BROUGHT YOU JOY TODAY?
_____
_____
_____

WHAT ARE YOU HOPEFUL FOR IN THE FUTURE?
_____
_____
_____

WHAT IS SOMETHING AROUND YOU RIGHT NOW THAT YOU APPRECIATE?
_____
_____
_____

GRATITUDE IS A DAILY DECISION.

SMALL JOYS OFTEN HOLD THE BIGGEST MEANING.

WHAT DO YOU ENJOY MOST ABOUT YOUR JOB OR CREATIVE WORK?

WHAT'S A COMFORT ITEM THAT MAKES YOU FEEL GOOD?

WHAT'S A RECENT MOMENT THAT MADE YOU LAUGH?

WHAT IS A DREAM YOU'VE ACHIEVED THAT ONCE FELT IMPOSSIBLE?

WHAT DOES A "GOOD DAY" LOOK LIKE TO YOU?

THE BEST MOMENTS ARE MADE OF LITTLE THINGS.

A GRATEFUL MIND SEES ENDLESS POSSIBILITIES.

WHAT OPPORTUNITY ARE YOU THANKFUL YOU TOOK?

WHAT DO YOU LOVE MOST ABOUT YOUR MORNING OR EVENING ROUTINE?

WHAT HOBBY OR ACTIVITY ARE YOU THANKFUL FOR?

WHO BELIEVES IN YOUR DREAMS EVEN WHEN YOU DOUBT THEM?

WHAT MADE TODAY MEANINGFUL?

GRATITUDE MAKES SIMPLE MOMENTS EXTRAORDINARY.

HAPPINESS GROWS WHERE GRATITUDE LIVES.

WHAT SKILL OR TALENT ARE YOU PROUD TO HAVE?

WHAT'S YOUR FAVORITE WAY TO RELAX AND UNWIND?

WHAT MEMORY ALWAYS MAKES YOU SMILE?

WHAT'S ONE GOAL YOU'RE EXCITED TO WORK TOWARD?

WHAT ARE THREE THINGS THAT MADE YOU FEEL SAFE OR SUPPORTED?

GIVE THANKS FOR WHAT YOU HAVE— AND WATCH IT GROW.

DATE
_____

TODAY'S LITTLE JOYS ARE TOMORROW'S BIG MEMORIES.

WHAT LESSON HAVE YOU LEARNED FROM FAILURE?
_____
_____
_____

WHAT SCENT, SOUND, OR SIGHT REMINDS YOU OF HOME?
_____
_____
_____

WHAT'S YOUR FAVORITE WAY TO CELEBRATE LIFE?
_____
_____
_____

WHAT DO YOU LOVE ABOUT THE PERSON YOU'RE BECOMING?
_____
_____
_____

WHAT ARE YOU GRATEFUL FOR... THAT YOU DIDN'T NOTICE UNTIL NOW?
_____
_____
_____

APPRECIATION IS A QUIET KIND OF POWER.

THE MORE YOU NOTICE,
THE MORE YOU'LL APPRECIATE.

WHAT INCONVENIENCE TURNED OUT TO BE A BLESSING IN DISGUISE?

_____

_____

_____

WHAT DAILY ITEM OR TOOL MAKES YOUR LIFE EASIER?

_____

_____

_____

WHAT'S A RECENT KIND WORD SOMEONE SAID TO YOU?

_____

_____

_____

WHAT CAN YOUR BODY DO THAT YOU'RE THANKFUL FOR?

_____

_____

_____

WHAT CREATIVE OUTLET BRINGS YOU JOY?

_____

_____

_____

EVERY ACT OF GRATITUDE CREATES A BETTER WORLD.

DATE

WHERE GRATITUDE FLOWS, POSITIVITY GROWS.

WHAT'S SOMETHING YOU DIDN'T ENJOY AT FIRST BUT ARE NOW GRATEFUL FOR?

_____

_____

_____

WHAT SMALL CHORE DO YOU FEEL THANKFUL TO BE ABLE TO DO?

_____

_____

_____

WHAT MEMORY DO YOU TREASURE WITH SOMEONE YOU LOVE?

_____

_____

_____

HOW HAVE YOU CARED FOR YOUR HEALTH THIS WEEK?

_____

_____

_____

WHAT'S SOMETHING YOU'VE MADE THAT YOU'RE PROUD OF?

_____

_____

_____

THERE'S MAGIC IN MINDFUL THANKFULNESS.

DATE _____

A SINGLE MOMENT OF THANKS CAN BRIGHTEN AN ENTIRE DAY.

WHAT SURPRISE THIS MONTH BROUGHT YOU UNEXPECTED JOY?

_____

_____

_____

WHAT'S YOUR FAVORITE PART OF YOUR MORNING RITUAL?

_____

_____

_____

WHAT DO YOU APPRECIATE MOST ABOUT YOUR CLOSEST FRIEND?

_____

_____

_____

WHAT ACTIVITY MAKES YOU FEEL ALIVE AND STRONG?

_____

_____

_____

WHAT INSPIRES YOU TO CREATE OR IMAGINE?

_____

_____

_____

GRATITUDE IS YOUR SUPERPOWER.

COUNT YOUR BLESSINGS, NOT YOUR BURDENS.

WHAT DO YOU TAKE FOR GRANTED THAT DESERVES MORE APPRECIATION?

_____

_____

_____

WHAT DO YOU ENJOY ABOUT YOUR COMMUTE, WALK, OR ERRANDS?

_____

_____

_____

WHAT'S SOMETHING THOUGHTFUL SOMEONE DID WITHOUT BEING ASKED?

_____

_____

_____

WHAT'S ONE HEALTHY CHOICE YOU MADE RECENTLY?

_____

_____

_____

WHAT BOOK, MOVIE, OR SONG ARE YOU GRATEFUL FOR?

_____

_____

_____

NOTICE THE GOOD, AND YOU'LL SEE MORE OF IT.

DATE

THE HEART THAT GIVES THANKS IS ALWAYS FULL.

WHEN WAS THE LAST TIME A DELAY WORKED OUT IN YOUR FAVOR?

WHAT'S A REGULAR RESPONSIBILITY YOU'RE GLAD YOU CAN HANDLE?

WHO IN YOUR LIFE SUPPORTS YOU UNCONDITIONALLY?

WHAT'S SOMETHING YOUR SENSES HELPED YOU ENJOY TODAY?

WHAT IDEA OR DAYDREAM MAKES YOU FEEL HOPEFUL?

A MOMENT OF GRATITUDE IS A PAUSE FOR JOY.

GRATITUDE DOESN'T CHANGE THINGS—
IT CHANGES YOU.

WHAT'S SOMETHING YOU LOVED AS A CHILD THAT YOU STILL APPRECIATE?

_____

_____

WHAT LIMITING BELIEF HAVE YOU OVERCOME?

_____

_____

WHAT'S SOMETHING YOU'RE LOOKING FORWARD TO IN THE NEXT WEEK?

_____

_____

WHAT'S SOMETHING FREE THAT BRINGS YOU JOY?

_____

_____

WHAT'S SOMETHING YOU'VE RECENTLY FORGIVEN YOURSELF FOR?

_____

_____

_____

GRATEFUL HEARTS CREATE GRATEFUL HOMES.

THERE IS ALWAYS SOMETHING TO BE THANKFUL FOR.

WHAT WAS A HAPPY MOMENT FROM YOUR TEENAGE YEARS?

WHAT HELPS YOU STAY OPTIMISTIC DURING CHALLENGES?

WHAT PAST DREAM ARE YOU LIVING NOW?

WHAT SMALL LUXURY DO YOU TREAT YOURSELF TO?

WHAT PAST MISTAKE HELPED YOU BECOME WISER?

THE ART OF LIVING BEGINS WITH APPRECIATION.

FIND JOY IN THE ORDINARY.

WHAT DID YOU LEARN IN THE PAST YEAR THAT CHANGED YOUR PERSPECTIVE?

_____

_____

_____

WHAT BRINGS YOU PEACE WHEN THINGS FEEL UNCERTAIN?

_____

_____

_____

WHO CHEERS YOU ON, NO MATTER WHAT?

_____

_____

_____

WHAT DO YOU LOVE ABOUT A COZY EVENING AT HOME?

_____

_____

_____

WHAT'S SOMETHING YOU'RE PROUD OF, EVEN IF NO ONE ELSE KNOWS?

_____

_____

_____

WHEN YOU FOCUS ON THE GOOD, THE GOOD GETS BETTER.

DATE _____

GRATEFUL THOUGHTS BUILD A JOYFUL LIFE.

HOW HAS YOUR DEFINITION OF GRATITUDE CHANGED OVER TIME?

_____

_____

WHAT MANTRA OR PHRASE KEEPS YOU GROUNDED?

_____

_____

WHAT'S SOMETHING THAT REMINDS YOU TO DREAM BIG?

_____

_____

WHAT'S YOUR FAVORITE SIMPLE MEAL OR SNACK?

_____

_____

WHAT DOES "ENOUGH" MEAN TO YOU TODAY?

_____

_____

_____

THE ART OF LIVING BEGINS WITH APPRECIATION.

DATE

PAUSE. BREATHE. APPRECIATE.

WHAT OLD HABIT ARE YOU THANKFUL TO HAVE OUTGROWN?

_____

_____

WHAT ARE YOU LEARNING TO LET GO OF?

_____

_____

WHAT FUTURE POSSIBILITY EXCITES YOU MOST?

_____

_____

WHAT DO YOU ENJOY ABOUT YOUR CURRENT WEATHER?

_____

_____

WHAT DO YOU LOVE MOST ABOUT YOUR LIFE RIGHT NOW?

_____

_____

_____

GRATITUDE MAKES THE SOUL SHINE.

DATE _____

A GRATEFUL SOUL IS A PEACEFUL SOUL.

WHAT MADE YOU SMILE TODAY?
_____
_____
_____

WHO HAS MADE A POSITIVE IMPACT IN YOUR LIFE RECENTLY?
_____
_____
_____

WHAT PERSONAL STRENGTH HAVE YOU RELIED ON THIS WEEK?
_____
_____
_____

WHAT NATURAL PLACE BRINGS YOU PEACE?
_____
_____
_____

WHAT'S YOUR FAVORITE TIME OF DAY AND WHY?
_____
_____
_____

WHAT IF TODAY, WE WERE
JUST GRATEFUL FOR EVERYTHING?

DATE
_____

SAYING "THANK YOU" CREATES A RIPPLE OF KINDNESS.

WHAT'S SOMETHING YOU CAN HEAR RIGHT NOW THAT BRINGS COMFORT?
_____
_____

WHO DO YOU FEEL SAFE AROUND, AND WHY?
_____
_____
_____

WHAT'S SOMETHING YOU'VE ACCOMPLISHED THAT FELT MEANINGFUL?
_____
_____
_____

WHAT'S YOUR FAVORITE SEASON AND WHY?
_____
_____
_____

WHAT HOUSEHOLD ITEM ARE YOU GLAD TO HAVE?
_____
_____
_____

A SMILE IS A SILENT WAY TO SAY, "I'M GRATEFUL."

DATE

NOT EVERY DAY IS GOOD,
BUT THERE'S GOOD IN EVERY DAY.

WHAT MOMENT TODAY FELT PEACEFUL OR CALM?

WHO INSPIRES YOU TO BE YOUR BEST SELF?

WHAT'S A SKILL OR TALENT YOU'RE GRATEFUL TO HAVE?

WHAT NATURAL SOUNDS HELP YOU RELAX?

WHAT SCENT TRIGGERS A HAPPY MEMORY?

THE SMALLEST THANKS IS BETTER THAN
THE GREATEST INTENTION.

DATE
_____

GRATITUDE HELPS YOU SEE
WHAT'S ALREADY BEAUTIFUL.

WHAT FOOD OR DRINK ARE YOU THANKFUL FOR TODAY?
_____
_____
_____

WHO DO YOU ADMIRE, AND WHAT DO YOU ADMIRE ABOUT THEM?
_____
_____
_____

WHAT HABIT HAVE YOU DEVELOPED THAT SUPPORTS YOUR WELL-BEING?
_____
_____
_____

WHAT OUTDOOR MEMORY BRINGS A SMILE TO YOUR FACE?
_____
_____
_____

WHAT'S A RECENT MEAL OR SNACK YOU TRULY ENJOYED?
_____
_____
_____

GRATITUDE GIVES US FRESH EYES FOR FAMILIAR JOYS.

THANKFULNESS IS THE QUICKEST PATH TO JOY.

WHAT ARE YOU LOOKING AT RIGHT NOW THAT YOU APPRECIATE?

_____

_____

WHAT'S A RECENT CONVERSATION THAT LEFT YOU FEELING GRATEFUL?

_____

_____

WHAT'S A CHALLENGE YOU'VE GROWN FROM RECENTLY?

_____

_____

WHAT'S YOUR FAVORITE FLOWER, PLANT, OR TREE?

_____

_____

WHAT'S A COZY SPACE IN YOUR HOME YOU'RE THANKFUL FOR?

_____

_____

_____

CHOOSE THANKFULNESS—IT'S ALWAYS IN STYLE.

DATE _____

A GRATEFUL HEART SEES
LIGHT IN THE DARKEST TIMES.

WHAT DIFFICULT MOMENT HELPED YOU DISCOVER YOUR STRENGTH?

_____

_____

_____

WHAT BOOK, ARTICLE, OR PODCAST TAUGHT YOU SOMETHING NEW?

_____

_____

_____

WHAT MODERN CONVENIENCE DO YOU APPRECIATE MOST?

_____

_____

_____

WHAT CHOICE HAVE YOU MADE RECENTLY THAT YOU'RE PROUD OF?

_____

_____

_____

WHAT QUALITY IN YOURSELF ARE YOU MOST GRATEFUL FOR?

_____

_____

_____

COLLECT MOMENTS, NOT THINGS.

DATE _____

THE MORE GRATEFUL YOU ARE,
THE RICHER YOUR LIFE BECOMES.

WHAT'S SOMETHING HARD THAT YOU MADE IT THROUGH?

_____
_____
_____

WHAT SUBJECT OR TOPIC FASCINATES YOU?

_____
_____
_____

WHAT ITEM IN YOUR HOME BRINGS YOU COMFORT?

_____
_____
_____

WHAT DID YOU INTENTIONALLY SAY NO TO THAT PROTECTED YOUR PEACE?

_____
_____
_____

WHAT'S SOMETHING NICE YOU DID FOR SOMEONE ELSE RECENTLY?

_____
_____
_____

APPRECIATION IS THE ANTIDOTE TO STRESS.

DATE

THE HABIT OF BEING THANKFUL
LEADS TO CONTENTMENT.

WHAT SUPPORT HELPED YOU DURING A TOUGH TIME?

WHAT'S A MISTAKE YOU LEARNED FROM?

WHAT DO YOU LOVE MOST ABOUT YOUR FAVORITE PIECE OF CLOTHING?

WHAT SMALL ACT OF SELF-CARE DID YOU PRACTICE TODAY?

WHAT MAKES YOU UNIQUE THAT YOU GENUINELY VALUE?

JOY HIDES IN MOMENTS WE USUALLY OVERLOOK.

THANKFULNESS UNLOCKS JOY IN THE MUNDANE.

WHAT LESSON DID YOU LEARN FROM A RECENT MISTAKE?

_____

_____

WHAT'S SOMETHING YOU'RE EXCITED TO LEARN MORE ABOUT?

_____

_____

WHAT'S SOMETHING SOFT, WARM, OR COZY YOU'RE GRATEFUL FOR?

_____

_____

WHAT BOUNDARY ARE YOU GRATEFUL YOU'VE SET?

_____

_____

WHAT'S A TRAIT OR BEHAVIOR YOU'VE WORKED HARD TO IMPROVE?

_____

_____

_____

LIFE IS BRIGHTER THROUGH A THANKFUL LENS.

LIFE'S SWEETNESS IS FOUND IN ITS SIMPLEST GIFTS.

WHAT PAST DISAPPOINTMENT ARE YOU NOW THANKFUL FOR?

WHAT'S A RECENT "AHA" MOMENT YOU HAD?

WHAT MAKES YOUR DAILY LIFE EASIER?

WHAT'S SOMETHING YOU DID TODAY JUST FOR YOURSELF?

WHAT COMPLIMENTS ARE YOU LEARNING TO BELIEVE?

CHOOSE GRATITUDE, ESPECIALLY WHEN IT'S HARD.

DATE _____

LET GRATITUDE ANCHOR YOUR HEART.

WHAT CHILDHOOD MEMORY ARE YOU GRATEFUL FOR?

_____
_____

WHAT'S AN EVENT THAT BROUGHT YOU JOY THIS YEAR?

_____
_____

WHAT EMOTION DID YOU FEEL TODAY THAT YOU'RE THANKFUL FOR?

_____
_____

WHO SHOWED YOU KINDNESS RECENTLY?

_____
_____

WHAT PART OF YOUR MORNING ROUTINE DO YOU LOOK FORWARD TO?

_____
_____
_____

LET APPRECIATION LEAD YOU HOME.

SOMETIMES, THE QUIETEST THANKS
ARE THE LOUDEST.

WHAT WAS A TURNING POINT IN YOUR LIFE YOU'RE THANKFUL FOR?

_____

_____

_____

WHAT EXPERIENCE PUSHED YOU OUTSIDE YOUR COMFORT ZONE?

_____

_____

_____

WHEN WAS THE LAST TIME YOU FELT DEEPLY CONTENT?

_____

_____

_____

WHO DO YOU APPRECIATE BUT HAVEN'T TOLD YET?

_____

_____

_____

WHAT DO YOU ENJOY ABOUT YOUR COMMUTE OR TRAVEL TIME?

_____

_____

_____

GRATITUDE CREATES SPACE FOR PEACE.

DATE _____

SAVOR THE NOW—IT'S ALL WE REALLY HAVE.

WHO FROM YOUR PAST TAUGHT YOU A VALUABLE LIFE LESSON?

_____

_____

_____

WHAT'S A MOMENT YOU'LL ALWAYS TREASURE?

_____

_____

_____

WHAT HELPS YOU FEEL EMOTIONALLY SUPPORTED?

_____

_____

_____

WHAT IS A RECENT COMPLIMENT YOU RECEIVED?

_____

_____

_____

WHAT DID YOU OVERLOOK THAT YOU ARE NOW THANKFUL FOR?

_____

_____

_____

A GRATEFUL MOMENT BEATS A PERFECT ONE.

BEING GRATEFUL CHANGES THE TONE
OF YOUR WHOLE DAY.

WHAT'S A TRIP YOU TOOK THAT CHANGED YOUR PERSPECTIVE?

WHAT'S A HOBBY OR ACTIVITY THAT BRINGS YOU HAPPINESS?

WHAT RECENT MOMENT GAVE YOU A SENSE OF AWE OR WONDER?

WHO DO YOU TURN TO WHEN YOU NEED ENCOURAGEMENT?

WHAT DAILY RITUAL BRINGS CALM TO YOUR LIFE?

YOU'LL FIND WHAT YOU FOCUS ON—
CHOOSE GRATITUDE.

YOU DON'T NEED MORE—YOU NEED TO NOTICE MORE.

WHAT'S SOMETHING YOU'VE KEPT FROM YOUR PAST THAT HOLDS MEANING?

WHAT'S A TIME YOU LAUGHED UNCONTROLLABLY?

WHAT'S A WAY YOU'VE SHOWN YOURSELF COMPASSION RECENTLY?

WHAT'S A SHARED MEMORY WITH A LOVED ONE THAT MAKES YOU SMILE?

WHAT'S A TOOL OR APP THAT HELPS KEEP YOU ORGANIZED?

THE BEST WAY TO GROW HAPPINESS IS TO WATER WITH GRATITUDE.

DATE

GRATITUDE IS A SUNRISE FOR THE SOUL.

WHAT MOTIVATES YOU TO KEEP GOING?

WHAT DO YOU APPRECIATE ABOUT YOUR HOME?

WHAT INCONVENIENCE TURNED OUT TO BE A BLESSING?

WHAT ARE YOU EXCITED ABOUT IN THE NEXT WEEK?

WHAT'S SOMETHING SIMPLE THAT MADE TODAY FEEL SPECIAL?

GRATITUDE CREATES BEAUTY FROM THE INSIDE OUT.

DATE _____

APPRECIATE TODAY—IT WILL NEVER COME AGAIN.

WHAT'S A RECENT DECISION YOU'RE GLAD YOU MADE?

_____

_____

WHAT'S A SOUND THAT BRINGS YOU PEACE?

_____

_____

_____

WHAT MISTAKE TAUGHT YOU SOMETHING ESSENTIAL?

_____

_____

_____

WHAT GOAL ARE YOU GRATEFUL TO BE WORKING TOWARD?

_____

_____

_____

WHAT COLOR OR TEXTURE ARE YOU THANKFUL FOR TODAY?

_____

_____

_____

YOU'RE SURROUNDED BY MORE GOODNESS THAN YOU THINK.

A GRATEFUL SPIRIT IS A RESILIENT ONE.

WHAT PERSONAL BOUNDARY HAS HELPED YOU FEEL HEALTHIER?

WHAT'S SOMETHING IN YOUR NEIGHBORHOOD YOU'RE GRATEFUL FOR?

WHAT DETOUR IN LIFE LED TO SOMETHING BETTER?

WHAT IS SOMETHING YOU'RE WAITING FOR THAT FILLS YOU WITH HOPE?

WHAT'S A SMALL ACT OF KINDNESS YOU NOTICED?

SOMETIMES, SAYING "THANK YOU" IS ALL YOU NEED.

DATE _____

GRATITUDE SLOWS TIME IN THE BEST WAY.

WHAT PART OF YOUR PERSONALITY DO YOU FEEL MOST GRATEFUL FOR?

_____

_____

WHAT'S YOUR FAVORITE WEATHER, AND WHY?

_____

_____

WHAT SURPRISE MADE YOU SMILE RECENTLY?

_____

_____

WHAT INTENTION WOULD YOU LIKE TO CARRY INTO TOMORROW?

_____

_____

WHAT'S SOMETHING ABOUT THIS MOMENT THAT BRINGS CALM?

_____

_____

_____

GRATITUDE IS FREE—AND PRICELESS.

LET YOUR HEART SAY THANK YOU MORE OFTEN.

WHAT'S SOMETHING YOU'VE FORGIVEN YOURSELF FOR?

_____

_____

_____

WHAT PART OF YOUR CITY OR TOWN FEELS SPECIAL TO YOU?

_____

_____

_____

WHAT UNPLANNED MOMENT ARE YOU THANKFUL FOR?

_____

_____

_____

WHAT DO YOU HOPE TO FEEL MORE OF IN THE FUTURE?

_____

_____

_____

WHAT'S SOMETHING YOU'RE GRATEFUL FOR THAT YOU DIDN'T EXPECT?

_____

_____

_____

LOOK FOR THINGS TO APPRECIATE—
THEY'RE EVERYWHERE.

DATE _____

THE ROAD TO PEACE IS PAVED WITH THANKFULNESS.

WHAT MADE YOU SMILE UNEXPECTEDLY TODAY?

_____

_____

_____

WHO MADE YOU FEEL VALUED RECENTLY?

_____

_____

_____

WHAT'S SOMETHING YOU NOTICED TODAY THAT YOU USUALLY OVERLOOK?

_____

_____

_____

WHAT'S A HARD SITUATION THAT HELPED YOU GROW?

_____

_____

_____

WHAT'S A SMALL WIN FROM THIS WEEK?

_____

_____

_____

FIND BEAUTY IN WHAT YOU ALREADY HAVE.

GRATEFULNESS TURNS ROUTINE INTO RITUAL.

WHAT SONG LIFTED YOUR SPIRITS RECENTLY?

WHAT CONVERSATION MEANT A LOT TO YOU?

WHAT ARE YOU GRATEFUL FOR IN THIS VERY MOMENT?

WHAT FEAR HAVE YOU OVERCOME?

WHAT'S A HABIT YOU'RE GLAD YOU STARTED?

LET GO OF LACK, LEAN INTO THANKS.

NOTICE THE TINY JOYS—THEY ADD UP FAST.

WHAT'S A SMALL JOY YOU EXPERIENCED THIS WEEK?

WHO CONSISTENTLY SHOWS UP FOR YOU?

WHAT'S A SOUND, SCENT, OR TASTE THAT BRINGS COMFORT?

WHAT'S A RECENT CHALLENGE YOU'RE PROUD OF FACING?

WHAT'S A GOAL YOU'VE MADE PROGRESS ON?

YOUR HEART KNOWS THE WAY— THROUGH GRATITUDE.

DATE _____

BEING PRESENT IS A FORM OF GRATITUDE.

WHAT DO YOU LOOK FORWARD TO EACH MORNING?

_____

_____

WHAT'S A LOVING GESTURE SOMEONE MADE TOWARD YOU?

_____

_____

HOW DID YOU SLOW DOWN TODAY?

_____

_____

WHAT'S SOMETHING YOU ONCE STRUGGLED WITH BUT NOW HANDLE WELL?

_____

_____

HOW HAVE YOU GROWN OVER THE PAST YEAR?

_____

_____

_____

GIVE THANKS OFTEN AND OUT LOUD.

DATE

GRATITUDE MAKES YOUR LIFE GLOW.

WHAT'S SOMETHING FUN YOU DID JUST FOR YOURSELF?

WHAT'S ONE THING YOU APPRECIATE ABOUT SOMEONE YOU'RE CLOSE WITH?

WHAT'S SOMETHING BEAUTIFUL YOU SAW RECENTLY?

WHAT MINDSET SHIFT HAS HELPED YOU RECENTLY?

WHAT ARE YOU BETTER AT TODAY THAN YOU WERE SIX MONTHS AGO?

THERE IS ALWAYS SOMETHING WORTH SMILING ABOUT.

YOU ARE RICH IN WAYS MONEY CAN'T BUY.

WHAT FOOD BROUGHT YOU COMFORT RECENTLY?

_____

_____

WHAT PART OF NATURE DO YOU FEEL DRAWN TO?

_____

_____

WHAT CREATIVE OUTLET ARE YOU THANKFUL FOR?

_____

_____

WHAT TOOL OR ROUTINE HELPS YOU STAY GROUNDED?

_____

_____

WHAT ARE YOU EXCITED TO CREATE OR EXPERIENCE NEXT?

_____

_____

_____

WHAT YOU APPRECIATE, APPRECIATES.

DATE _____

EVEN SMALL STEPS DESERVE CELEBRATION.

WHAT'S YOUR FAVORITE COZY SPOT AT HOME?

_____

_____

WHAT'S YOUR FAVORITE SEASON, AND WHY?

_____

_____

WHAT IDEA HAS RECENTLY SPARKED YOUR CURIOSITY?

_____

_____

WHAT KIND OF SELF-CARE MADE A DIFFERENCE THIS WEEK?

_____

_____

WHAT DREAM ARE YOU HOLDING SPACE FOR?

_____

_____

_____

A GRATEFUL SOUL IS A GENTLE ONE.

DATE

BEGIN WITH GRATITUDE, AND THE REST WILL FOLLOW.

WHAT'S YOUR FAVORITE PART OF YOUR NIGHTTIME ROUTINE?

_____

_____

_____

WHAT'S SOMETHING IN THE NATURAL WORLD YOU'RE GRATEFUL FOR TODAY?

_____

_____

_____

WHAT BOOK, PODCAST, OR ARTICLE INSPIRED YOU?

_____

_____

_____

WHAT'S SOMETHING YOU'VE LET GO OF THAT HAS IMPROVED YOUR LIFE?

_____

_____

_____

WHAT DO YOU WANT TO FEEL MORE OF IN THE COMING MONTHS?

_____

_____

_____

GRATITUDE IS THE MUSIC OF THE HEART.

GRATITUDE TRANSFORMS YOUR MINDSET, NOT JUST YOUR MOOD.

WHAT PIECE OF CLOTHING OR BLANKET MAKES YOU FEEL SAFE?

WHAT'S A FAVORITE PLACE TO WALK, HIKE, OR RELAX OUTDOORS?

WHAT'S SOMETHING YOU CREATED THAT MADE YOU PROUD?

WHAT BOUNDARIES HAVE MADE YOUR LIFE BETTER?

WHAT'S SOMETHING YOU'RE HOPEFUL ABOUT RIGHT NOW?

LIVE LESS FROM HABIT, MORE FROM THANKS.

DATE

LET YOUR THANKFULNESS OUTSHINE YOUR WORRIES.

WHAT'S A HOUSEHOLD ITEM YOU'RE THANKFUL FOR?

HOW DOES TIME OUTSIDE HELP YOU RESET?

WHAT TOPIC WOULD YOU LOVE TO EXPLORE MORE?

WHAT QUOTE OR MANTRA HELPS YOU STAY CENTERED?

WHAT'S A WAY YOU'D LIKE TO EXPRESS MORE GRATITUDE GOING FORWARD?

THANKFULNESS IS A KIND OF COURAGE.

A GRATEFUL MIND IS A GARDEN OF CALM.

WHAT'S SOMETHING THAT MADE TODAY EASIER?

WHO SURPRISED YOU WITH KINDNESS?

WHAT'S A PART OF YOURSELF YOU'VE GROWN TO LOVE?

WHAT'S A CHILDHOOD MEMORY YOU'RE THANKFUL FOR?

WHAT PART OF YOUR WORK BRINGS YOU JOY OR PURPOSE?

BE STILL. BE THANKFUL. BE YOU.

DATE

THE MORE YOU GIVE THANKS, THE MORE JOY YOU FIND.

WHAT MOMENT TODAY FELT MOST PEACEFUL?

WHO HAS TAUGHT YOU A VALUABLE LIFE LESSON?

WHAT PERSONAL STRENGTH DO YOU RELY ON?

WHAT DID SOMEONE LONG AGO DO THAT SHAPED YOU?

WHAT PROJECT HAVE YOU FELT PROUD TO COMPLETE?

GRATITUDE BRINGS COLOR TO THE GRAYSCALE DAYS.

NOTICE THE BEAUTY IN THE PAUSE.

WHAT HELPED YOU STAY GROUNDED TODAY?

WHO HAS MADE YOU FEEL SAFE?

WHAT'S SOMETHING YOU'VE FORGIVEN YOURSELF FOR?

WHAT'S A LIFE MILESTONE YOU'RE GRATEFUL TO HAVE EXPERIENCED?

WHO AT WORK HAS MADE YOUR DAY BETTER?

THE WORLD CHANGES
WHEN WE CHOOSE TO SEE THE GOOD.

DATE

_____

APPRECIATION IS A PRACTICE, NOT A MOMENT.

WHAT DID YOU SAVOR WITH YOUR SENSES TODAY?

_____

_____

_____

WHAT'S SOMETHING A STRANGER DID THAT MADE A DIFFERENCE?

_____

_____

_____

WHAT COMPLIMENTS HAVE YOU RECEIVED THAT MEANT A LOT?

_____

_____

_____

WHAT LESSON FROM THE PAST ARE YOU STILL USING TODAY?

_____

_____

_____

WHAT SKILL ARE YOU GLAD YOU LEARNED?

_____

_____

_____

GRATITUDE MAKES YOUR STORY WORTH REREADING.

DATE _____

YOUR BLESSINGS ARE BIGGER THAN YOUR PROBLEMS.

WHAT MOMENT ARE YOU GRATEFUL HAPPENED EXACTLY AS IT DID?

_____

_____

_____

WHO MADE YOU LAUGH RECENTLY?

_____

_____

_____

HOW HAVE YOU HONORED YOUR NEEDS RECENTLY?

_____

_____

_____

WHAT'S A PLACE FROM YOUR PAST THAT HOLDS MEANING?

_____

_____

_____

HOW HAS YOUR WORK TAUGHT YOU TO GROW?

_____

_____

_____

YOU ARE ENOUGH—
AND THAT'S WORTH CELEBRATING.

SHINE BRIGHTER WITH THANKS.

WHAT ARE YOU LEARNING ABOUT YOURSELF RIGHT NOW?

WHAT DAILY RITUAL DO YOU LOVE?

WHAT'S SOMETHING YOUR BODY HAS DONE FOR YOU LATELY?

WHAT TRIP OR JOURNEY ARE YOU THANKFUL FOR?

WHAT SMELL INSTANTLY MAKES YOU FEEL HAPPY?

THANKS IS THE SOUL'S SUNSHINE.

DATE

TODAY IS A GIFT—UNWRAP IT WITH JOY.

WHAT REALIZATION HAS BROUGHT YOU PEACE?

WHAT MORNING HABIT HELPS START YOUR DAY RIGHT?

WHAT MOVEMENT OR EXERCISE MAKES YOU FEEL GOOD?

WHAT DESTINATION BROUGHT YOU A SENSE OF AWE?

WHAT ITEM IN YOUR HOME HAS A SPECIAL STORY?

BE AMAZED BY THE ORDINARY.

PEACE BLOOMS WHERE GRATITUDE GROWS.

WHAT DO YOU KNOW NOW THAT YOU DIDN'T LAST YEAR?

WHAT EVENING ROUTINE HELPS YOU RELAX?

WHAT'S A HEALTH IMPROVEMENT YOU'RE PROUD OF?

WHAT HAVE YOU LEARNED FROM TRAVELING OR EXPLORING NEW PLACES?

WHAT QUOTE OR PHRASE DO YOU TURN TO OFTEN?

THANKS UNLOCKS THE PRESENT MOMENT.

THANKFULNESS TURNS A MOMENT INTO A MEMORY.

HOW HAVE YOUR VALUES GUIDED YOUR CHOICES?

WHAT TRADITION BRINGS YOU COMFORT OR JOY?

WHAT'S SOMETHING YOU DO THAT HELPS YOU SLEEP BETTER?

WHAT'S A CULTURAL EXPERIENCE THAT SHAPED YOU?

WHAT'S A RECENT COINCIDENCE YOU'RE GRATEFUL FOR?

LOOK FOR THE GOOD— IT'S ALWAYS HIDING SOMEWHERE.

DATE

LET YOUR ATTITUDE BE ONE OF GRATITUDE.

WHAT'S SOMETHING YOU'VE SAID "NO" TO—AND BEEN GRATEFUL FOR?

WHAT'S A SEASONAL RITUAL YOU LOOK FORWARD TO?

WHAT NOURISHING FOOD ARE YOU GRATEFUL FOR?

WHAT TRAVEL MEMORY WOULD YOU LOVE TO RELIVE?

WHAT TINY THING MADE A BIG IMPACT ON YOUR DAY?

GRATEFUL EYES SEE BEAUTY FIRST.

EACH BREATH IS A QUIET GIFT.

WHAT DID YOU TAKE FOR GRANTED THAT YOU NOW APPRECIATE?

WHAT PART OF YOUR DAY DO YOU LOOK FORWARD TO MOST?

WHAT ITEM BRINGS YOU DAILY COMFORT?

WHAT'S A DIFFICULT TIME YOU'RE GRATEFUL TO HAVE GOTTEN THROUGH?

WHAT PART OF NATURE ARE YOU MOST DRAWN TO?

BREATHE IN APPRECIATION. BREATHE OUT JOY.

JOY AND GRATITUDE WALK HAND IN HAND.

HOW HAS YOUR MINDSET SHIFTED FOR THE BETTER?

_____

_____

_____

WHAT RECENT MOMENT MADE YOU FEEL TRULY PRESENT?

_____

_____

_____

WHAT SMALL LUXURY MAKES YOU SMILE?

_____

_____

_____

WHAT'S SOMETHING YOU'VE OVERCOME THAT YOU'RE PROUD OF?

_____

_____

_____

WHAT OUTDOOR SPACE FEELS LIKE A SANCTUARY?

_____

_____

_____

DON'T RUSH THROUGH THE MAGIC.

DATE

WHEN IN DOUBT, START WITH THANKS.

WHAT'S A CHALLENGE YOU NOW SEE AS A GIFT?

WHAT'S SOMETHING YOU NOTICED TODAY YOU MIGHT'VE MISSED BEFORE?

WHAT'S A COMFORTING SOUND OR SCENT YOU LOVE?

WHAT MISTAKE TAUGHT YOU SOMETHING IMPORTANT?

WHAT'S A FAVORITE MEMORY IN NATURE?

A THANKFUL LIFE IS A BEAUTIFUL ONE.

DATE _____

GRATITUDE ADDS LIGHTNESS TO LIVING.

WHAT HELPS YOU STAY HOPEFUL?

_____

_____

_____

WHAT'S A WAY YOU PAUSED TO ENJOY THE MOMENT?

_____

_____

_____

WHAT MEAL OR SNACK BRINGS YOU JOY?

_____

_____

_____

HOW HAVE YOU GROWN EMOTIONALLY IN THE LAST YEAR?

_____

_____

_____

WHAT'S A RECENT MOMENT OUTDOORS YOU'RE GRATEFUL FOR?

_____

_____

_____

GRATITUDE IS THE HEARTBEAT OF JOY.

DATE

APPRECIATE YOUR NOW—
IT'S LEADING TO YOUR NEXT.

WHAT SMALL CHOICE HAD A BIG IMPACT?

WHAT'S SOMETHING YOU SLOWED DOWN TO APPRECIATE?

WHAT MAKES YOUR HOME FEEL LIKE HOME?

WHAT COPING STRATEGY ARE YOU THANKFUL YOU DISCOVERED?

WHAT DO YOU LOVE MOST ABOUT THE CHANGING SEASONS?

THE WORLD IS BRIGHTER THROUGH GRATEFUL EYES.

DATE

BE GRATEFUL FOR HOW FAR YOU'VE COME.

WHAT CREATIVE OUTLET ARE YOU GRATEFUL FOR?

WHAT PERSONAL WIN DID YOU CELEBRATE RECENTLY?

WHAT'S SOMETHING YOU LET GO OF THAT IMPROVED YOUR LIFE?

WHAT UNEXPECTED GIFT CAME YOUR WAY?

WHAT PART OF YOUR LIFE JOURNEY ARE YOU THANKFUL FOR?

GRATITUDE IS THE BEST WAY TO BEGIN ANYTHING.

DATE

A GRATEFUL DAY IS A GREAT DAY.

WHAT PROJECT MADE YOU FEEL ALIVE?

WHAT MILESTONE WAS MORE MEANINGFUL THAN YOU EXPECTED?

WHAT NEGATIVE HABIT OR BELIEF HAVE YOU RELEASED?

WHAT HAPPY SURPRISE MADE YOUR DAY?

WHAT'S A "DETOUR" YOU'RE NOW GRATEFUL HAPPENED?

SAVOR THE SIMPLE.

THANKFULNESS CREATES MOMENTUM.

HOW DO YOU EXPRESS YOURSELF MOST AUTHENTICALLY?

WHAT'S A MOMENT YOU WANT TO REMEMBER FOREVER?

WHAT DID YOU STOP DOING THAT BROUGHT RELIEF?

WHAT COINCIDENCE FELT MEANINGFUL?

WHAT CHAPTER OF YOUR LIFE BROUGHT UNEXPECTED JOY?

THANKS ISN'T JUST A WORD—IT'S A PERSPECTIVE.

DATE

_____

YOU'RE MORE BLESSED THAN YOU FEEL TODAY.

_____

WHAT PIECE OF ART, MUSIC, OR WRITING MOVED YOU?

_____

_____

_____

WHAT ARE YOU PROUD OF HAVING STARTED?

_____

_____

_____

WHAT'S SOMETHING YOU'RE LEARNING TO FORGIVE?

_____

_____

_____

WHAT UNEXPECTED COMPLIMENT UPLIFTED YOU?

_____

_____

_____

WHAT DIRECTION ARE YOU THANKFUL YOU DIDN'T TAKE?

_____

_____

_____

LIVE IN WONDER. LIVE IN THANKS.

DATE

YOUR BEST DAYS BEGIN WITH GRATITUDE.

WHAT INSPIRES YOUR CREATIVITY?

WHAT HAS EXCEEDED YOUR EXPECTATIONS LATELY?

WHAT'S NO LONGER WEIGHING YOU DOWN?

WHAT'S A DETOUR THAT LED SOMEWHERE BETTER?

WHAT'S A REMINDER THAT YOU'RE ON THE RIGHT PATH?

GROW ROOTS IN GRATITUDE.

GRATITUDE GIVES YOUR LIFE DIMENSION.

WHO IS SOMEONE THAT HAS MADE YOUR LIFE BETTER JUST BY BEING IN IT?

WHAT DO YOU LOVE TO DO WHEN NO ONE IS WATCHING?

WHAT'S SOMETHING NEW YOU'VE LEARNED RECENTLY?

WHAT HELPS YOU FEEL RECHARGED?

WHAT MOTIVATES YOU TO KEEP GOING ON HARD DAYS?

NOTHING IS TOO SMALL TO BE APPRECIATED.

BE THANKFUL. NOT FOR EVERYTHING,
BUT IN EVERYTHING.

WHAT RECENT ACT OF KINDNESS FROM SOMEONE ARE YOU THANKFUL FOR?

WHAT'S A SOLO ACTIVITY THAT BRINGS YOU PEACE?

WHAT SUBJECT OR TOPIC EXCITES YOU?

WHAT'S A HABIT THAT'S IMPROVED YOUR WELL-BEING?

WHO OR WHAT INSPIRES YOU RIGHT NOW?

GRATITUDE IS CLARITY FOR THE SOUL.

DATE
_____

A FULL HEART LEAVES NO ROOM FOR FEAR.

WHO DO YOU FEEL MOST YOURSELF AROUND?
_____
_____
_____

WHAT'S A RECENT MOMENT YOU HAD ALL TO YOURSELF?
_____
_____
_____

WHAT'S A MISTAKE THAT HELPED YOU GROW?
_____
_____
_____

WHAT'S A SMALL SELF-CARE RITUAL THAT BRINGS COMFORT?
_____
_____
_____

WHAT QUOTE OR PHRASE STICKS WITH YOU?
_____
_____
_____

LET YOUR LIFE BE A THANK YOU.

THANKS IS THE LANGUAGE OF ABUNDANCE.

WHO ENCOURAGES YOU WHEN YOU'RE FEELING DOWN?

WHAT HOBBY FEELS LIKE THERAPY?

WHAT SKILL ARE YOU GRATEFUL TO HAVE LEARNED?

WHAT MAKES YOU FEEL STRONGEST IN YOUR BODY?

WHAT'S SOMETHING YOU'VE DONE THAT ONCE SCARED YOU?

THE SMALLEST THINGS
OFTEN LEAVE THE BIGGEST MARK.

DATE _____

LET EVERY "THANK YOU" ECHO THROUGH YOUR LIFE.

WHAT'S A COMPLIMENT YOU'LL ALWAYS REMEMBER?

_____

_____

_____

WHAT MAKES A DAY FEEL RESTFUL FOR YOU?

_____

_____

_____

WHAT DO YOU ENJOY RESEARCHING OR READING ABOUT?

_____

_____

_____

WHAT'S YOUR FAVORITE WAY TO UNWIND?

_____

_____

_____

WHAT ARE YOU EXCITED TO TRY NEXT?

_____

_____

_____

YOU'LL FIND WHAT YOU'RE LOOKING FOR—
LOOK FOR GOOD.

CHOOSE TO SEE THE GIFT IN EVERY MOMENT.

WHAT'S A SMALL, BEAUTIFUL DETAIL YOU NOTICED TODAY?

WHAT'S A CONVERSATION THAT MEANT A LOT TO YOU?

WHAT'S A LITTLE WIN YOU'RE PROUD OF?

WHAT DO YOU LOVE MOST ABOUT YOUR HOME?

WHAT'S ONE THING YOU CAN DO TODAY TO SHOW GRATITUDE?

A LIFE WELL LIVED IS ONE WELL NOTICED.

A GRATEFUL MINDSET IS A CREATIVE ONE.

WHAT'S A RECENT SUNSET, FLOWER, OR SKY MOMENT YOU REMEMBER?

_____

_____

WHAT KIND OF CONNECTION DO YOU VALUE MOST?

_____

_____

WHAT'S THE LAST THING YOU CELEBRATED?

_____

_____

WHAT'S YOUR FAVORITE CORNER OR SPACE TO RELAX?

_____

_____

HOW DO YOU EXPRESS THANKS TO OTHERS?

_____

_____

THANKS ADDS SPARKLE TO THE DAY.

DATE _____

SEE THE WONDER IN THE FAMILIAR.

WHAT'S A BEAUTIFUL PLACE YOU'VE BEEN GRATEFUL TO SEE?

_____

_____

_____

WHAT'S A RECENT SHARED LAUGH OR INSIDE JOKE YOU'RE THANKFUL FOR?

_____

_____

_____

WHAT BRINGS OUT YOUR PLAYFUL SIDE?

_____

_____

_____

WHAT MAKES YOUR SPACE FEEL UNIQUELY YOURS?

_____

_____

_____

WHAT'S A SMALL WAY YOU'VE PAID IT FORWARD?

_____

_____

_____

THE WORLD CHANGES WHEN YOU APPRECIATE IT.

DATE

PRACTICE THANKS IN THE SMALLEST OF THINGS.

WHAT DOES BEAUTY MEAN TO YOU TODAY?

WHAT'S SOMETHING YOU APPRECIATE ABOUT TALKING WITH A FRIEND?

WHAT'S SOMETHING THAT MADE YOU LAUGH RECENTLY?

WHAT DO YOU ENJOY ABOUT YOUR NEIGHBORHOOD OR TOWN?

WHAT'S A WAY YOU'D LIKE TO GIVE BACK MORE OFTEN?

CHOOSE TO BE THANKFUL EVEN WHEN IT'S HARD.

DATE

YOU'RE LIVING A MOMENT
SOMEONE ELSE IS PRAYING FOR.

WHAT'S THE MOST PEACEFUL VIEW YOU'VE ENJOYED?

WHAT'S A MEMORY OF DEEP CONNECTION YOU HOLD CLOSE?

WHAT DO YOU ENJOY DOING JUST FOR FUN?

WHAT SOUNDS OR SMELLS MAKE YOU FEEL AT HOME?

HOW HAS PRACTICING GRATITUDE CHANGED HOW YOU ACT?

ONE GRATEFUL MOMENT CAN SHIFT YOUR MINDSET.

WHEN GRATITUDE LEADS, PEACE FOLLOWS.

WHAT'S SOMETHING YOU'RE PROUD OF ABOUT YOURSELF TODAY?

WHAT CREATIVE OUTLET BRINGS YOU JOY?

WHAT ARE YOU THANKFUL FOR RIGHT NOW, IN THIS MOMENT?

WHAT MAKES YOUR HOME FEEL LIKE HOME?

WHAT'S YOUR FAVORITE THING ABOUT THE CURRENT SEASON?

GRATITUDE IS THE ARTIST OF JOY.

DATE

LET GRATITUDE REWRITE YOUR STORY.

HOW HAVE YOU GROWN IN THE LAST YEAR?

WHEN DO YOU FEEL MOST INSPIRED?

WHAT'S SOMETHING SMALL THAT BROUGHT YOU JOY TODAY?

WHAT SMELLS OR SOUNDS REMIND YOU OF COMFORT?

WHAT OUTDOOR SPOT FILLS YOU WITH PEACE?

WHAT YOU NOTICE BECOMES WHAT YOU TREASURE.

DATE

A THANKFUL PAUSE CAN CHANGE YOUR WHOLE DAY.

WHAT'S A CHALLENGE THAT SHAPED WHO YOU ARE?

WHAT'S SOMETHING YOU'VE MADE THAT YOU'RE PROUD OF?

WHAT'S A CURRENT ROUTINE YOU'RE GRATEFUL FOR?

WHAT'S A ROUTINE AT HOME THAT YOU LOOK FORWARD TO?

WHAT'S A RECENT MOMENT YOU ENJOYED IN NATURE?

CONTENTMENT BLOOMS IN THANKFUL HEARTS.

DATE _____

GRATITUDE FINDS CALM IN CHAOS.

WHAT'S SOMETHING YOU LIKE ABOUT YOUR PERSONALITY?

_____

_____

_____

WHAT'S A FORM OF ART OR CREATIVITY YOU ADMIRE?

_____

_____

_____

WHAT ARE YOU APPRECIATING MORE AS YOU GET OLDER?

_____

_____

_____

WHAT'S A SIMPLE HOUSEHOLD ITEM YOU'RE THANKFUL FOR?

_____

_____

_____

WHAT DO YOU APPRECIATE ABOUT THE WEATHER TODAY?

_____

_____

_____

THE SMALL WINS ARE STILL WINS.

APPRECIATION IS THE MELODY OF THE SOUL.

WHAT PART OF YOUR DAILY ROUTINE MAKES YOU FEEL GROUNDED?

WHAT CREATIVE RISK ARE YOU THANKFUL YOU TOOK?

WHAT'S ONE THING TODAY THAT WENT BETTER THAN EXPECTED?

WHAT MAKES YOU FEEL SAFE AND SECURE?

WHAT NATURAL VIEW TAKES YOUR BREATH AWAY?

MAKE GRATITUDE YOUR DAILY RITUAL.

DATE

SAY THANK YOU TO THE LITTLE THINGS—
THEY BUILD THE BIG THINGS.

WHAT'S SOMETHING YOU ENJOY ABOUT YOUR WORK?

WHAT ORDINARY ITEM MAKES YOUR LIFE EASIER?

WHAT PAST STRUGGLE HELPS YOU APPRECIATE YOUR LIFE MORE NOW?

WHAT ARE YOU LOOKING FORWARD TO THIS WEEK?

WHAT HELPS YOU REMEMBER TO FEEL GRATEFUL?

YOU HOLD MORE LIGHT THAN YOU KNOW.

DATE _____

WHAT FILLS THE HEART SPILLS INTO THE DAY.

WHAT'S A CAREER ACHIEVEMENT YOU'RE PROUD OF?
_____
_____
_____

WHAT'S A MUNDANE TASK YOU ACTUALLY ENJOY?
_____
_____
_____

WHAT DO YOU SEE DIFFERENTLY AFTER PRACTICING GRATITUDE?
_____
_____
_____

WHAT'S A GOAL THAT EXCITES YOU RIGHT NOW?
_____
_____
_____

WHAT TIME OF DAY FEELS BEST TO REFLECT?
_____
_____
_____
_____

THANKS IS THE WHISPER OF JOY.

GRATITUDE SHINES THROUGH EVEN THE CRACKS.

WHAT TASK OR PROJECT HAVE YOU FELT DEEPLY INVESTED IN?

_____

_____

_____

WHAT IS A SOURCE OF JOY THAT YOU USED TO TAKE FOR GRANTED?

_____

_____

_____

WHAT'S A CHANGE IN MINDSET YOU'RE THANKFUL FOR?

_____

_____

_____

WHAT'S A DREAM YOU'RE GRATEFUL TO STILL HAVE?

_____

_____

_____

WHAT JOURNALING PRACTICE HELPS YOU FEEL CALM?

_____

_____

_____

NOTICE THE GRACE IN YOUR ROUTINE.

DATE
_____

A GRATEFUL MIND BUILDS A BRIGHTER FUTURE.

WHAT'S ONE SKILL YOU USE EVERY DAY THAT YOU'RE GRATEFUL TO HAVE?
_____
_____
_____

WHAT'S SOMETHING BORING THAT BRINGS YOU PEACE?
_____
_____
_____

WHAT'S SOMETHING YOU'VE LET GO OF THAT CREATED PEACE?
_____
_____
_____

WHAT POSSIBILITY ARE YOU HOPEFUL ABOUT?
_____
_____
_____

WHAT DOES WRITING ABOUT GRATITUDE DO FOR YOUR MOOD?
_____
_____
_____

BEING THANKFUL IS A WAY OF BEING BRAVE.

LET JOY SNEAK IN THROUGH A THANKFUL HEART.

WHO AT WORK HAS MADE YOUR DAY BETTER?

_____

_____

_____

WHAT'S A REGULAR OCCURRENCE THAT BRINGS YOU JOY?

_____

_____

_____

WHAT REMINDER BRINGS YOU BACK TO WHAT REALLY MATTERS?

_____

_____

_____

WHAT FUTURE MEMORY ARE YOU EXCITED TO CREATE?

_____

_____

_____

WHAT'S A SMALL RITUAL YOU'VE CREATED JUST FOR YOURSELF?

_____

_____

_____

GRATITUDE IS THE LENS THAT SEES CLEARLY.

GRATITUDE DOESN'T WAIT FOR PERFECTION.

WHAT HELPED YOU SLOW DOWN AND BE PRESENT TODAY?

WHAT COMMON TASK DO YOU APPRECIATE HAVING THE ABILITY TO DO?

WHO MADE YOU FEEL SEEN OR HEARD RECENTLY?

WHAT HABIT OR PRACTICE MAKES YOU FEEL RECHARGED?

WHAT TEACHER OR MENTOR MADE A DIFFERENCE IN YOUR LIFE?

THERE IS BEAUTY IN THE NOW—FIND IT.

THANKFULNESS BRINGS PERSPECTIVE AND PEACE.

WHAT SENSORY EXPERIENCE ARE YOU THANKFUL FOR?

WHAT'S A SMALL CONVENIENCE YOU'RE GRATEFUL EXISTS?

WHO IN YOUR LIFE BRINGS YOU JOY JUST BY BEING THEMSELVES?

HOW DID YOU TAKE CARE OF YOURSELF TODAY?

WHAT'S A MEMORY THAT MAKES YOU SMILE EVERY TIME?

EVEN A QUIET THANK YOU HAS POWER.

FIND JOY IN WHAT DIDN'T GO WRONG.

WHAT DID YOU NOTICE TODAY THAT YOU OFTEN OVERLOOK?

WHAT HOUSEHOLD ITEM MAKES YOUR LIFE EASIER?

WHAT COMPLIMENT OR KIND WORD DO YOU STILL REMEMBER?

WHAT'S SOMETHING YOUR BODY ALLOWED YOU TO DO TODAY?

WHAT'S A CHILDHOOD TRADITION YOU LOOK BACK ON FONDLY?

GRATEFUL HEARTS SEE BEAUTY IN THE MESS.

GRATITUDE IS THE ANCHOR IN ANY STORM.

WHAT QUIET MOMENT MADE YOU FEEL AT PEACE?

WHAT SIMPLE PLEASURE LIFTED YOUR SPIRITS TODAY?

WHO ARE YOU GRATEFUL TO HAVE IN YOUR SUPPORT SYSTEM?

WHAT'S A WAY YOU SHOWED YOURSELF COMPASSION THIS WEEK?

WHAT EVENT IN THE PAST DO YOU NOW APPRECIATE FOR ITS LESSONS?

BEGIN AND END YOUR DAY IN THANKS.

THANKS ISN'T JUST FOR GOOD DAYS—
IT'S FOR GROWTH.

WHAT'S ONE THING YOU ENJOYED DOING WITHOUT MULTITASKING?

WHAT'S A PART OF YOUR DAILY ROUTINE THAT YOU GENUINELY ENJOY?

WHAT'S A MOMENT OF LAUGHTER YOU SHARED WITH SOMEONE RECENTLY?

WHAT HELPS YOU FEEL EMOTIONALLY BALANCED?

WHAT DID YOU USED TO STRUGGLE WITH BUT HAVE NOW OVERCOME?

WHEN YOU'RE GRATEFUL,
EVERY STEP FEELS LIGHTER.

DATE

THE GIFT OF TODAY IS REASON ENOUGH.

WHAT'S SOMETHING YOU LEARNED RECENTLY THAT FASCINATED YOU?

WHAT INSPIRES YOU TO KEEP GROWING?

WHAT MOMENT RECENTLY LEFT YOU SPEECHLESS (IN A GOOD WAY)?

WHAT'S A SUNRISE, SUNSET, OR SKY YOU REMEMBER VIVIDLY?

WHAT IN YOUR CURRENT LIFE WOULD YOUR YOUNGER SELF BE EXCITED ABOUT?

GRATITUDE SOFTENS THE ROUGH EDGES OF LIFE.

GRATITUDE DEEPENS THE MEANING OF NOW.

WHAT BOOK, MOVIE, OR PODCAST LEFT A POSITIVE IMPACT ON YOU?

WHAT CURIOSITY HAVE YOU BEEN GRATEFUL TO FOLLOW?

WHAT UNEXPECTED JOY SURPRISED YOU THIS WEEK?

WHAT SKILL OR TALENT ARE YOU GRATEFUL TO HAVE DEVELOPED?

WHICH CONVERSATION LATELY INSPIRED YOU?

THANKFULNESS SHARPENS
YOUR VISION FOR THE GOOD.

DATE

THANKFULNESS IS A FORM OF QUIET STRENGTH.

WHAT'S A HOBBY OR INTEREST THAT MAKES LIFE MORE COLORFUL?

WHAT NATURAL BEAUTY HAVE YOU WITNESSED LATELY?

WHAT PLACE OR SETTING MAKES YOU FEEL INSTANTLY CALM?

WHAT WENT RIGHT TODAY THAT YOU MIGHT HAVE MISSED BEFORE?

WHAT SMELL IMMEDIATELY BRINGS BACK HAPPY MEMORIES?

YOU ARE SURROUNDED BY GIFTS—NOTICE THEM.

YEAR IN REVIEW
REFLECT ON YOUR GOALS

THINGS I DID WELL

_____
_____
_____
_____
_____
_____
_____
_____
_____
_____
_____
_____

THINGS I SHOULD STOP

_____
_____
_____
_____
_____
_____
_____
_____
_____
_____
_____
_____

YEAR IN REVIEW
REFLECT ON YOUR GOALS

THINGS I SHOULD IMPROVE

_____
_____
_____
_____
_____
_____
_____
_____
_____

THINGS I SHOULD TRY

_____
_____
_____
_____
_____
_____
_____
_____
_____
_____

www.ingramcontent.com/pod-product-compliance
Lightning Source LLC
Chambersburg PA
CBHW050541280326
41933CB00011B/1677